YOUR SAFE BODY

WRITTEN AND ILLUSTRATED BY
KATIE HASTINGS, RN

ISBN 978-1-66783-180-0

eBook ISBN 978-1-66783-181-7

PARENTS' FOREWORD

Studies show before the age of 18, one in three girls, and one in five boys are sexually abused. Studies also show that 95% of sexual abuse is preventable through education. Many thanks to you for supporting this cause!

SHOUT™:

S is for **Stop**

H is for **Help**

O is for **Out**

U is for **Unsafe**

T is for **Tell**

The world is a wonderful, beautiful place.

There are mountains, deserts, beaches,
forests, oceans, rivers, lakes, and streams.

There are animals, bugs, plants, trees, flowers, and food.

There's a big blue sky, a sun, and a moon.

And along with many, many people
in this world...

There's you!

You have a body. Bodies are incredible! Everyone is unique and special in their own way, but something we all have in common is a body.

Most bodies have two eyes that can see, two ears that can hear, and a nose that can smell.

Two hands that can
grab and hold things.
Two legs and two feet
that can walk, skip, hop
and run. Ten fingers
and ten toes that can
wiggle in the sand.

But best of all every human body has a brain. Your brain helps you think, make decisions, and gives you a wonderful personality!

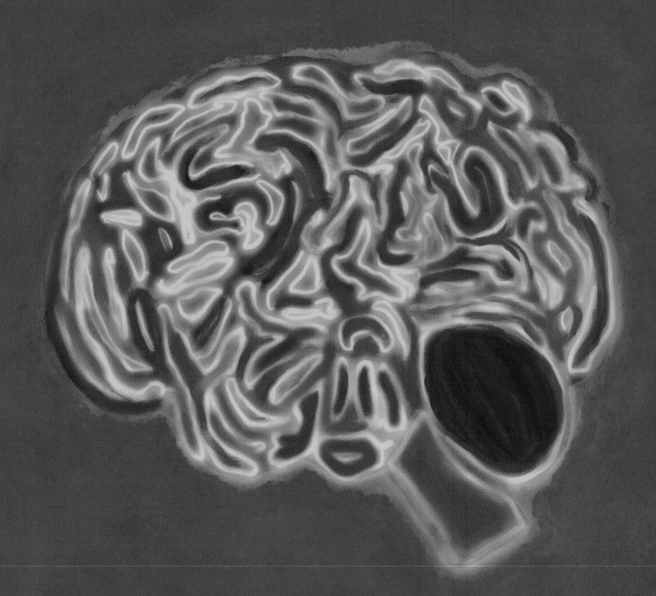

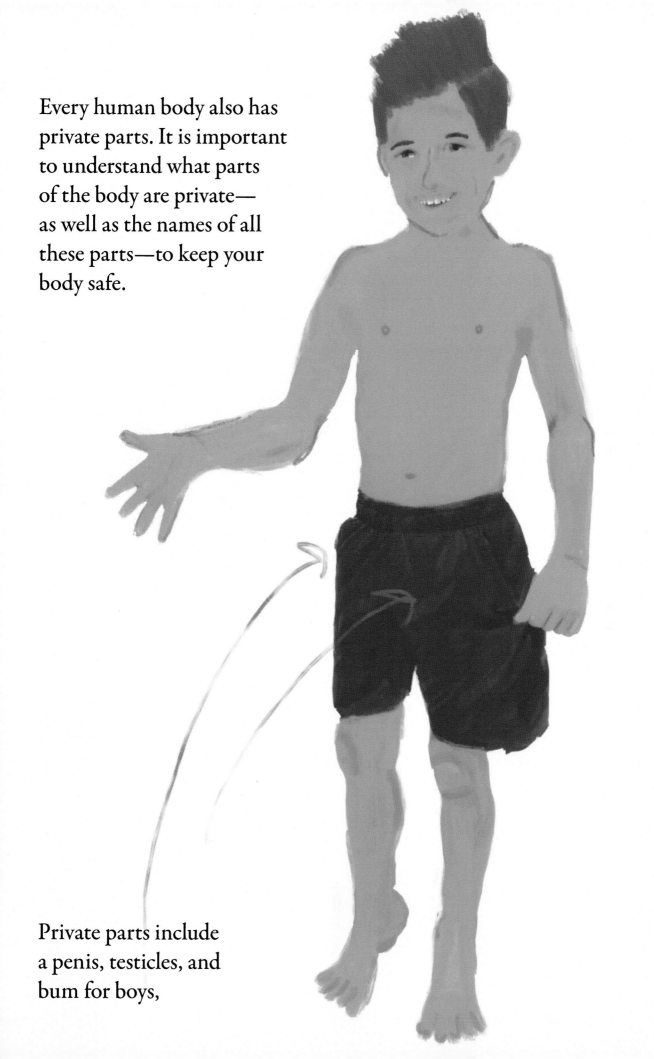

Every human body also has private parts. It is important to understand what parts of the body are private— as well as the names of all these parts—to keep your body safe.

Private parts include a penis, testicles, and bum for boys,

and a vulva, vagina, bum and
breasts for girls.

When you are young,
the main purpose of
these parts is to help
you go to the
bathroom.
When you are
older, they help
you reproduce.

But private parts are special and should not be touched often the same way you touch your hands, face, feet, toes or nose.

They should be treated differently because they are personal. To keep private parts personal, do not allow others to touch or look at them without permission.

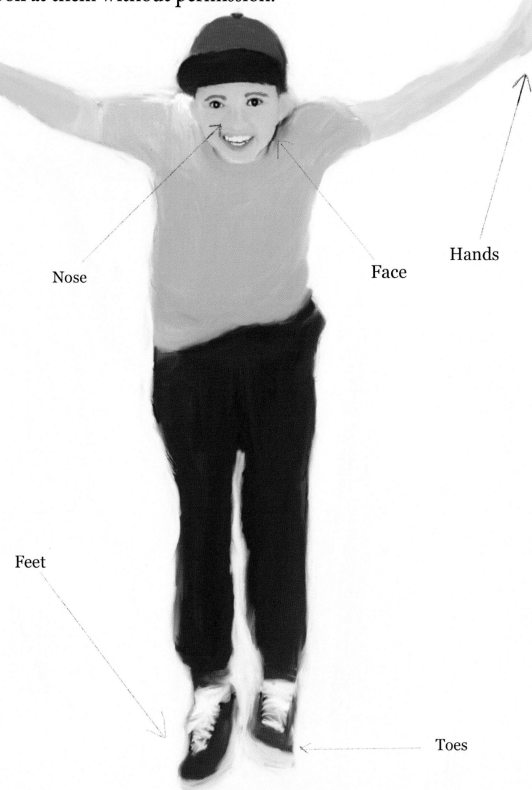

Nose

Face

Hands

Feet

Toes

An adult you trust can help you with things like
getting dressed, going potty, or bathing. Sometimes
a mom, dad, or safe adult may need to help you when
your private parts might be seen.

But only when you need help,
and when you say it is okay.

You can do things to protect your body, like wearing a helmet when you ride a bike, or a seatbelt when in the car.

You can also learn ways to keep private parts personal, like knowing **SHOUT.**

S is for Stop

H is for Help

O is for Out

U is for Unsafe

T is for Tell

Keeping your body and private parts safe is a big job, but you can do it!

You can shout, **"STOP,"** anytime you feel uncomfortable!
Even with friends, family, other children, or adults—because
you are in charge of your body.

If you do not want someone to touch your private parts, you can shout,
"STOP!" If you do not want someone to look at your private parts,
you can shout, **"STOP!"**

If someone is trying to show you their private parts,
you can shout, **"STOP!"**

When you shout stop, you can shout, **"HELP"** at the same time.
If no one is around, you know you need to find **HELP** from a trusted
parent or adult.

If you are able to leave where you are, get **OUT**, go home, or go somewhere you feel safe as soon as you can.

Anyone not listening when you shout, "stop," is being **UNSAFE**.
Anyone who wants you to look at, or touch their private parts is being **UNSAFE**.

You should also **TELL** a trusted adult what happened that made you shout, stop!

If anyone has ever looked at or touched your private parts, has shown you their private parts, or asked you to touch their private parts, now is a good time to **TELL** your parents, or a trusted adult. They will know how to help you!

You may feel embarrassed, or worried you will get in trouble if you **TELL.** Remember you are not in trouble when you **TELL** a trusted adult what happened.

You have a wonderful
body that can do so
many wonderful things!
Remember **SHOUT!**
You can keep your body
safe by keeping your
private parts personal.

Stop

Help

Out

Unsafe

Tell

SHOUT